FOREWORD

The collection of "Everything Will Be Okay" travel phrasebooks published by T&P Books is designed for people traveling abroad for tourism and business. The phrasebooks contain what matters most - the essentials for basic communication. This is an indispensable set of phrases to "survive" while abroad.

This phrasebook will help you in most cases where you need to ask something, get directions, find out how much something costs, etc. It can also resolve difficult communication situations where gestures just won't help.

This book contains a lot of phrases that have been grouped according to the most relevant topics. You'll also find a mini dictionary with useful words - numbers, time, calendar, colors…

Take "Everything Will Be Okay" phrasebook with you on the road and you'll have an irreplaceable traveling companion who will help you find your way out of any situation and teach you to not fear speaking with foreigners.

TABLE OF CONTENTS

T&P Books Publishing

T&P Books Publishing

PHRASEBOOK
BELARUSIAN

THE MOST IMPORTANT PHRASES

This phrasebook contains
the most important
phrases and questions
for basic communication
Everything you need
to survive overseas

T&P
BOOKS

By Andrey Taranov

Phrasebook + 250-word dictionary

English-Belarusian phrasebook & mini dictionary

By Andrey Taranov

The collection of "Everything Will Be Okay" travel phrasebooks published by T&P Books is designed for people traveling abroad for tourism and business. The phrasebooks contain what matters most - the essentials for basic communication. This is an indispensable set of phrases to "survive" while abroad.

You'll also find a mini dictionary with 250 useful words required for everyday communication - the names of months and days of the week, measurements, family members, and more.

T&P Books Publishing
www.tpbooks.com

ISBN: 978-1-80001-569-2

This book is also available in E-book formats.
Please visit www.tpbooks.com or the major online bookstores.

PRONUNCIATION

Letter	Belarusian example	T&P phonetic alphabet	English example
А а	Англія	[a]	shorter than in ask
Б б	бульба	[b]	baby, book
В в	вечар	[v]	very, river
Г г	галава	[ɦ]	between [g] and [h]
Д д	дзіця	[d]	day, doctor
Дж дж	джаз	[ʤ]	joke, general
Е е	метр	[ɛ]	man, bad
Ё ё	вясёлы	[jɔ]	New York
Ж ж	жыццё	[ʒ]	forge, pleasure
З з	заўтра	[z]	zebra, please
І і	нізкі	[i]	shorter than in feet
Й й	англійскі	[j]	yes, New York
К к	красавік	[k]	clock, kiss
Л л	лінія	[l]	lace, people
М м	камень	[m]	magic, milk
Н н	Новы год	[n]	name, normal
О о	опера	[ɔ]	bottle, doctor
П п	піва	[p]	pencil, private
Р р	морква	[r]	rice, radio
С с	соль	[s]	city, boss
Т т	трус	[t]	tourist, trip
У у	ізумруд	[u]	book
Ў ў	каўбаса	[w]	vase, winter
Ф ф	футра	[f]	face, food
Х х	захад	[h]	home, have
Ц ц	цэнтр	[ts]	cats, tsetse fly
Ч ч	пачатак	[ʧ], [ɕ]	church, French
Ш ш	штодня	[ʃ]	machine, shark
Ь ь	попельніца	[ʲ]	soft sign - no sound
Ы ы	рыжы	[ɨ]	big, America
'	сузор'е	[ˮ]	hard sign, no sound
Э э	Грэцыя	[ɛ]	man, bad
Ю ю	плюс	[ʉ]	youth, usually
Я я	трусяня	[ja], [ʲa]	royal

Letter	Belarusian example	T&P phonetic alphabet	English example

Combinations of letters

дз	дзень	[dz]	beads, kids
дзь	лебедзь	[ʣ]	jeans, gene
дж	джаз	[ʤ]	joke, general

LIST OF ABBREVIATIONS

English abbreviations

ab.	-	about
adj	-	adjective
adv	-	adverb
anim.	-	animate
as adj	-	attributive noun used as adjective
e.g.	-	for example
etc.	-	et cetera
fam.	-	familiar
fem.	-	feminine
form.	-	formal
inanim.	-	inanimate
masc.	-	masculine
math	-	mathematics
mil.	-	military
n	-	noun
pl	-	plural
pron.	-	pronoun
sb	-	somebody
sing.	-	singular
sth	-	something
v aux	-	auxiliary verb
vi	-	intransitive verb
vi, vt	-	intransitive, transitive verb
vt	-	transitive verb

Belarusian abbreviations

ж	-	feminine noun
ж мн	-	feminine plural
м	-	masculine noun
м мн	-	masculine plural
м, ж	-	masculine, feminine
мн	-	plural
н	-	neuter
н мн	-	neuter plural

T&P BOOKS

BELARUSIAN
PHRASEBOOK

This section contains
important phrases that may
come in handy in various
real-life situations.
The phrasebook will help
you ask for directions, clarify
a price, buy tickets, and
order food at a restaurant

T&P Books Publishing

PHRASEBOOK
CONTENTS

T&P Books Publishing

The bare minimum

Excuse me, …	**Прабачце, …** [pra'batʃse, …]
Hello.	**Прывітанне.** [privi'tanne.]
Thank you.	**Дзякуй.** [dzʲakuj.]
Good bye.	**Да пабачэння.** [da paba'tʃɛnnʲa.]
Yes.	**Так.** [tak.]
No.	**Не.** [ne.]
I don't know.	**Я ня ведаю.** [ˈʲa nʲa 'vedau̯.]
Where? | Where to? | When?	**Дзе? | Куды? | Калі?** [dze? | ku'dɨ? | ka'li?]

I need …	**Мне трэба …** [mne 'trɛba …]
I want …	**Я хачу …** [ˈʲa ha'tʃu …]
Do you have …?	**У вас ёсць …?** [u vas ʲostsʲ …?]
Is there a … here?	**Тут ёсць …?** [tut ʲostsʲ …?]
May I …?	**Я магу …?** [ˈʲa ma'ɦu …?]
…, please (polite request)	**Калі ласка** [ka'li 'laska]

I'm looking for …	**Я шукаю …** [ˈʲa ʃu'kau̯ …]
the restroom	**туалет** [tua'let]
an ATM	**банкамат** [banka'mat]
a pharmacy (drugstore)	**аптэку** [ap'tɛku]
a hospital	**бальніцу** [balʲ'nitsu]
the police station	**аддзяленне міліцыі** [adzʲa'lenne mi'litsɨi]
the subway	**метро** [me'trɔ]

a taxi	**таксі** [tak'si]
the train station	**вакзал** [vak'zal]

My name is …	**Мяне завуць …** [mʲa'ne za'vutsʲ …]
What's your name?	**Як вас завуць?** [ʲak vas za'vutsʲ?]
Could you please help me?	**Дапамажыце мне, калі ласка.** [dapama'ʒitse mne, ka'li 'laska?]
I've got a problem.	**У мяне праблема.** [u mʲa'ne prab'lema.]
I don't feel well.	**Мне дрэнна.** [mne 'drɛnna.]
Call an ambulance!	**Выклікайце хуткую дапамогу!** [viklikajtse 'hutkuʉ dapa'mɔɦu!]
May I make a call?	**Магу я пазваніць?** [ma'ɦu ʲa pazva'nitsʲ?]

I'm sorry.	**Выбачце.** [vibatʃtse.]
You're welcome.	**Калі ласка.** [ka'li 'laska.]

I, me	**я** [ʲa]
you (inform.)	**ты** [ti]
he	**ён** [ʲon]
she	**яна** [ʲa'na]
they (masc.)	**яны** [ʲa'ni]
they (fem.)	**яны** [ʲa'ni]
we	**мы** [mi]
you (pl)	**вы** [vi]
you (sg, form.)	**вы** [vɨ]

ENTRANCE	**УВАХОД** [uva'hɔd]
EXIT	**ВЫХАД** [vihad]
OUT OF ORDER	**НЕ ПРАЦУЕ** [ne pra'tsue]
CLOSED	**ЗАЧЫНЕНА** [za'tʃinena]

OPEN	**АДЧЫНЕНА** [at'ʧinena]
FOR WOMEN	**ДЛЯ ЖАНЧЫН** [dlʲa ʒan'ʧin]
FOR MEN	**ДЛЯ МУЖЧЫН** [dlʲa muʒ'ʧin]

Questions

Where?	Дзе? [dze?]
Where to?	Куды? [ku'di?]
Where from?	Адкуль? [at'kulʲ?]
Why?	Чаму? [ʧa'mu?]
For what reason?	Навошта? [na'voʃta?]
When?	Калі? [ka'li?]

How long?	Як доўга? [ʲak 'dowɦa?]
At what time?	У колькі ? [u 'kolʲki?]
How much?	Колькі каштуе? [kolʲki kaʃ'tue?]
Do you have ...?	У вас ёсць ...? [u vas ʲostsʲ ...?]
Where is ...?	Дзе знаходзіцца ...? [dze zna'ɦodzitsa ...?]

What time is it?	Колькі часу? [kolʲki 'ʧasu?]
May I make a call?	Магу я пазваніць? [ma'ɦu ʲa pazva'nitsʲ?]
Who's there?	Хто там? [hto tam?]
Can I smoke here?	Тут дазволена курыць? [tut daz'volena ku'ritsʲ?]
May I ...?	Я магу ...? [ʲa ma'ɦu ...?]

Needs

I'd like …	**Я б хацеў /хацела/ …** ['a b ha'tsew /ha'tsela/ …]
I don't want …	**Я не хачу …** ['a ne ha'ʧu …]
I'm thirsty.	**Я хачу піць.** ['a ha'ʧu pitsʲ.]
I want to sleep.	**Я хачу спаць.** ['a ha'ʧu spatsʲ.]
I want …	**Я хачу …** ['a ha'ʧu …]
to wash up	**памыцца** [pa'mitsa]
to brush my teeth	**пачысціць зубы** [pa'ʧisʲtsitsʲ 'zubi]
to rest a while	**крыху адпачыць** [krihu adpa'ʧitsʲ]
to change my clothes	**пераапрануцца** [peraapra'nutsa]
to go back to the hotel	**вярнуцца ў гасцініцу** [vʲar'nutsa w ɦasʲ'tsinitsu]
to buy …	**купіць …** [ku'pitsʲ …]
to go to …	**з'ездзіць у …** [z'ezdzitsʲ u …]
to visit …	**наведаць …** [na'vedatsʲ …]
to meet with …	**сустрэцца з …** [sus'trɛtsa z …]
to make a call	**пазваніць** [pazva'nitsʲ]
I'm tired.	**Я стаміўся /стамілася/.** ['a sta'miwsʲa /sta'milasʲa/.]
We are tired.	**Мы стаміліся.** [mi sta'milisʲa.]
I'm cold.	**Мне холадна.** [mne 'ɦoladna.]
I'm hot.	**Мне горача.** [mne 'ɦoraʧa.]
I'm OK.	**Мне нармальна.** [mne nar'malʲna.]

I need to make a call.

Мне трэба пазваніць.
[mne 'trɛba pazva'nitsʲ.]

I need to go to the restroom.

Мне трэба ў туалет.
[mne 'trɛba w tua'let.]

I have to go.

Мне трэба ісці.
[mne 'trɛba is'tsi.]

I have to go now.

Мне трэба ісці.
[mne 'trɛba is'tsi.]

Asking for directions

Excuse me, …	**Прабачце, …** [pra'batʃtse, …]
Where is …?	**Дзе знаходзіцца …?** [dze zna'hodzitsa …?]
Which way is …?	**У якім напрамку знаходзіцца …?** [u ˈaˈkim naˈpramku znaˈhoditsa …?]
Could you help me, please?	**Дапамажыце мне, калі ласка.** [dapamaˈʒitse mne, kaˈli ˈlaska.]

I'm looking for …	**Я шукаю …** [ˈʲa ʃuˈkaʉ …]
I'm looking for the exit.	**Я шукаю выхад.** [ˈʲa ʃuˈkaʉ ˈvihad.]
I'm going to …	**Я еду ў …** [ˈʲa ˈedu w …]
Am I going the right way to …?	**Ці правільна я іду …?** [ˈtsi ˈpravilʲna ˈʲa idu …?]

Is it far?	**Гэта далёка?** [ˈhɛta daˈlʲoka?]
Can I get there on foot?	**Я дайду туды пешшу?** [ˈʲa dajˈdu tuˈdɨ ˈpeʃu?]
Can you show me on the map?	**Пакажыце мне на карце, калі ласка.** [pakaˈʒitse mne na karˈtse, kaˈli ˈlaska.]
Show me where we are right now.	**Пакажыце, дзе мы зараз.** [pakaˈʒitse, dze mɨ ˈzaraz.]

Here	**Тут** [tut]
There	**Там** [tam]
This way	**Сюды** [sʉˈdɨ]

Turn right.	**Павярніце направа.** [pavʲarˈnitse naˈprava.]
Turn left.	**Павярніце налева** [pavʲarˈnitse naˈleva]
first (second, third) turn	**першы (другі, трэці) паварот** [perʃɨ (druˈhi, ˈtrɛtsi) pavaˈrɔt]
to the right	**направа** [naˈprava]

to the left

налева
[na'leva]

Go straight ahead.

Ідзіце прама.
[i'dzitse 'prama.]

Signs

WELCOME!	**САРДЭЧНА ЗАПРАШАЕМ!** [sar'dɛʧna zapra'ʃaem!]
ENTRANCE	**УВАХОД** [uva'hɔd]
EXIT	**ВЫХАД** [vihad]
PUSH	**АД СЯБЕ** [at sʲa'be]
PULL	**НА СЯБЕ** [na sʲa'be]
OPEN	**АДЧЫНЕНА** [at'ʧinena]
CLOSED	**ЗАЧЫНЕНА** [za'ʧinena]
FOR WOMEN	**ДЛЯ ЖАНЧЫН** [dlʲa ʒan'ʧin]
FOR MEN	**ДЛЯ МУЖЧЫН** [dlʲa muʒ'ʧin]
GENTLEMEN, GENTS	**МУЖЧЫНСКІ ТУАЛЕТ** [muʒ'ʧinski tua'let]
WOMEN	**ЖАНОЧЫ ТУАЛЕТ** [ʒa'nɔʧi tua'let]
DISCOUNTS	**ЗНІЖКІ** [zniʒki]
SALE	**РАСПРОДАЖ** [ras'prɔdaʃ]
FREE	**БЯСПЛАТНА** [bʲas'platna]
NEW!	**НАВІНКА!** [na'vinka!]
ATTENTION!	**УВАГА!** [u'vaɦa!]
NO VACANCIES	**МЕСЦАЎ НЯМА** [mesʲtsaw nʲa'ma]
RESERVED	**ЗАРЭЗЕРВАВАНА** [zarɛzerva'vana]
ADMINISTRATION	**АДМІНІСТРАЦЫЯ** [admini'stratsʲʲa]
STAFF ONLY	**ТОЛЬКІ ДЛЯ ПЕРСАНАЛУ** [tolʲki dlʲa persa'nalu]

BEWARE OF THE DOG!

ЗЛЫ САБАКА
[zlі sa'baka]

NO SMOKING!

НЕ КУРЫЦЬ!
[ne ku'ritsʲl]

DO NOT TOUCH!

РУКАМІ НЕ КРАНАЦЬ!
[ru'kami ne kra'natsʲl]

DANGEROUS

НЕБЯСПЕЧНА
[nebʲa'spetʃna]

DANGER

НЕБЯСПЕКА
[nebʲa'speka]

HIGH VOLTAGE

ВЫСОКАЕ НАПРУЖАННЕ
[vɨ'sɔkae nap'ruʒanne]

NO SWIMMING!

КУПАЦЦА ЗАБАРОНЕНА
[ku'patsa zaba'rɔnena]

OUT OF ORDER

НЕ ПРАЦУЕ
[ne pra'tsue]

FLAMMABLE

ВОГНЕНЕБЯСПЕЧНА
[vɔfnenebʲas'petʃna]

FORBIDDEN

ЗАБАРОНЕНА
[zaba'rɔnena]

NO TRESPASSING!

ПРАХОД ЗАБАРОНЕНЫ
[pra'hɔd zaba'rɔneni]

WET PAINT

АФАРБАВАНА
[afarba'vana]

CLOSED FOR RENOVATIONS

ЗАЧЫНЕНА НА РАМОНТ
[za'tʃɨnena na ra'mɔnt]

WORKS AHEAD

РАМОНТНЫЯ РАБОТЫ
[ra'mɔntnɨʲa ra'bɔti]

DETOUR

АБ'ЕЗД
[a'bʲezt]

Transportation. General phrases

plane	самалёт [sama'ǉot]
train	цягнік [ts̪ah'nik]
bus	аўтобус [aw'tobus]
ferry	паром [pa'rɔm]
taxi	таксі [tak'si]
car	машына [ma'ʃina]
schedule	расклад руху [ras'klad 'ruhu]
Where can I see the schedule?	Дзе можна паглядзець расклад руху? [dze 'mɔʒna paɦǉa'dzets̪ʲ ras'klad 'ruhu?]
workdays (weekdays)	працоўныя дні [pra'ts̪ownʲia dni]
weekends	выхадныя дні [viɦad'nʲia dni]
holidays	святочныя дні [svʲa'tɔtʃnʲia dni]
DEPARTURE	АДПРАЎЛЕННЕ [adpraw'lenne]
ARRIVAL	ПРЫБЫЦЦЁ [pribi'ts̪ʲo]
DELAYED	ЗАТРЫМЛІВАЕЦЦА [za'trimlivaets̪a]
CANCELLED	АДМЕНЕНЫ [ad'menenɨ]
next (train, etc.)	наступны [na'stupni]
first	першы [perʃi]
last	апошні [a'pɔʃni]

When is the next ...?

Калі будзе наступны ...?
[ka'li 'budze na'stupni ...?]

When is the first ...?

Калі адыходзіць першы ...?
[ka'li adіhɔdzіʦ 'perʃі ...?]

When is the last ...?

Калі адыходзіць апошні ...?
[ka'li adіhɔdzіʦ a'pɔʃni ...?]

transfer (change of trains, etc.)

перасадка
[pera'satka]

to make a transfer

зрабіць перасадку
[zra'bіʦ pera'satku]

Do I need to make a transfer?

Мне патрэбна рабіць перасадку?
[mne pa'trɛbna ra'bіʦ pera'satku?]

Buying tickets

Where can I buy tickets?	**Дзе я магу купіць білеты?** [dze ʲa maˈɦu kuˈpitsʲ biˈleti?]
ticket	**білет** [biˈlet]
to buy a ticket	**купіць білет** [kuˈpitsʲ biˈlet]
ticket price	**кошт білета** [kɔʃt biˈleta]
Where to?	**Куды?** [kuˈdɨ?]
To what station?	**Да якой станцыі?** [da ʲaˈkɔj ˈstantsii?]
I need ...	**Мне трэба ...** [mne ˈtrɛba ...]
one ticket	**адзін білет** [aˈdzin biˈlet]
two tickets	**два білета** [dva biˈleta]
three tickets	**тры білета** [trɨ biˈleta]
one-way	**у адзін бок** [u aˈdzin bɔk]
round-trip	**туды і назад** [tuˈdɨ i naˈzad]
first class	**першы клас** [perʃɨ klas]
second class	**другі клас** [druˈɦi klas]
today	**сёння** [sʲonnʲa]
tomorrow	**заўтра** [zawtra]
the day after tomorrow	**паслязаўтра** [paslʲaˈzawtra]
in the morning	**раніцай** [ranitsaj]
in the afternoon	**удзень** [uˈdzenʲ]
in the evening	**увечары** [uˈvetʃarɨ]

aisle seat

месца ля праходу
[mesʲtsa lʲa praˈhɔdu]

window seat

месца ля вакна
[mesʲtsa lʲa vakˈna]

How much?

Колькі?
[kɔlʲki?]

Can I pay by credit card?

Магу я заплаціць карткай?
[maˈɦu ʲa zaplaˈtsitsʲ ˈkartkaj?]

Bus

bus	**аўтобус** [aw'tɔbus]
intercity bus	**міжгародны аўтобус** [miʒɦa'rɔdnɨ aw'tɔbus]
bus stop	**аўтобусны прыпынак** [aw'tɔbusnɨ prɨ'pɨnak]
Where's the nearest bus stop?	**Дзе бліжэйшы аўтобусны прыпынак?** [dze bli'ʒɛjʃɨ aw'tɔbusnɨ prɨ'pɨnak?]
number (bus ~, etc.)	**нумар** [numar]
Which bus do I take to get to ...?	**Які аўтобус ідзе да ...?** [ˈjaki aw'tɔbus i'dze da ...?]
Does this bus go to ...?	**Гэты аўтобус ідзе да ...?** [ɦɛtɨ aw'tɔbus i'dze da ...?]
How frequent are the buses?	**Як часта ходзяць аўтобусы?** [ˈjak 'tʃasta 'hɔdzʲatsʲ aw'tɔbusɨ?]
every 15 minutes	**кожныя пятнаццаць хвілін** [kɔʒnʲʲa pʲat'natsatsʲ hvi'lin]
every half hour	**кожныя паўгадзіны** [kɔʒnʲʲa pawɦa'dzinɨ]
every hour	**кожную гадзіну** [kɔʒnuɥ ɦa'dzinu]
several times a day	**некалькі разоў на дзень** [nekalʲki ra'zɔw na dzenʲ]
... times a day	**... раз на дзень** [... raz na dzenʲ]
schedule	**расклад руху** [ras'klad 'ruhu]
Where can I see the schedule?	**Дзе можна паглядзець расклад руху?** [dze 'mɔʒna paɦlʲʲa'dzetsʲ ras'klad 'ruhu?]
When is the next bus?	**Калі будзе наступны аўтобус?** [ka'li 'budze nas'tupnɨ aw'tɔbus?]
When is the first bus?	**Калі адыходзіць першы аўтобус?** [ka'li adɨ'hɔdzitsʲ 'perʃɨ aw'tɔbus?]
When is the last bus?	**Калі адыходзіць апошні аўтобус?** [ka'li adɨ'hɔdzitsʲ a'pɔʃni aw'tɔbus?]

stop

прыпынак
[pri'pinak]

next stop

наступны прыпынак
[na'stupni pri'pinak]

last stop (terminus)

канцавы прыпынак
[kantsa'vi pri'pinak]

Stop here, please.

Спыніце тут, калі ласка.
[spi'nitse tut, ka'li 'laska.]

Excuse me, this is my stop.

Дазвольце, гэта мой прыпынак.
[daz'volʲtse, 'hɛta mɔj pri'pinak.]

Train

train	**цягнік** [ts̪aɦ'nik]
suburban train	**прыгарадны цягнік** [priɦaradnɨ ts̪aɦ'nik]
long-distance train	**цягнік дальняга следавання** [ts̪aɦ'nik 'dalʲnʲaɦa 'sledavannʲa]
train station	**вакзал** [vak'zal]
Excuse me, where is the exit to the platform?	**Прабачце, дзе выхад да цягнікоў?** [pra'batʃtse, dze 'vɨhad da ts̪aɦni'kɔw?]
Does this train go to …?	**Гэты цягнік ідзе да …?** [ɦɛtɨ ts̪aɦ'nik i'dze da …?]
next train	**наступны цягнік** [na'stupnɨ ts̪aɦ'nik]
When is the next train?	**Калі будзе наступны цягнік?** [kali 'budze na'stupnɨ ts̪aɦ'nik?]
Where can I see the schedule?	**Дзе можна паглядзець расклад руху?** [dze 'mɔʒna paɦlʲa'dzetsʲ ras'klad 'ruhu?]
From which platform?	**Ад якой платформы?** [at ʲakɔj plat'fɔrmɨ?]
When does the train arrive in …?	**Калі цягнік прыбудзе ў …?** [kali ts̪aɦ'nik prɨ'budze w …?]
Please help me.	**Дапамажыце мне, калі ласка.** [dapama'ʒɨtse mne, ka'li 'laska.]
I'm looking for my seat.	**Я шукаю сваё месца.** [ʲa ʃu'kau svaʲo 'mesʲtsa.]
We're looking for our seats.	**Мы шукаем нашыя месцы.** [mɨ ʃu'kaem naʃʲa 'mesʲtsɨ.]
My seat is taken.	**Маё месца занята.** [maʲo 'mesʲtsa za'nʲata.]
Our seats are taken.	**Нашыя месцы заняты.** [naʃʲa 'mesʲtsɨ za'nʲatɨ.]
I'm sorry but this is my seat.	**Прабачце, калі ласка, але гэта маё месца.** [pra'batʃtse, ka'li 'laska, ale 'ɦɛta maʲo 'mesʲtsa.]

Is this seat taken?

Гэта месца свабодна?
[ɦɛta 'mesʲtsa sva'bɔdna?]

May I sit here?

Магу я тут сесці?
[ma'ɦu ʲa tut 'sesʲtsí?]

On the train. Dialogue (No ticket)

Ticket, please.	**Ваш білет, калі ласка.** [vaʃ bi'let, ka'li 'laska.]
I don't have a ticket.	**У мяне няма білета.** [u mʲa'ne nʲa'ma bi'leta.]
I lost my ticket.	**Я згубіў /згубіла/ свой білет.** [ʲa zɦu'biw /zɦu'bila/ svɔj bi'let.]
I forgot my ticket at home.	**Я забыўся /забылася/ білет дома.** [ʲa za'biwsʲa /za'bilasʲa/ bi'let 'dɔma.]

You can buy a ticket from me.	**Вы можаце купіць білет у мяне.** [vɨ 'mɔʒatse ku'pitsʲ bi'let u mʲa'ne.]
You will also have to pay a fine.	**Вам яшчэ давядзецца заплаціць штраф.** [vam ʲaɕɛ davʲa'dzɛtsa zapla'tsitsʲ 'ʃtraf.]
Okay.	**Добра.** [dɔbra.]
Where are you going?	**Куды вы едзеце?** [ku'dɨ vɨ 'edzetse?]
I'm going to …	**Я еду да …** [ʲa 'edu da …]

How much? I don't understand.	**Колькі? Я не разумею.** [kɔlʲki? ʲa ne razu'meʉ.]
Write it down, please.	**Напішыце, калі ласка.** [napi'ʃɨtse, ka'li 'laska.]
Okay. Can I pay with a credit card?	**Добра. Магу я заплаціць карткай?** [dɔbra. ma'ɦu ʲa zaplatsitsʲ 'kartkaj?]
Yes, you can.	**Так, можаце.** [tak, 'mɔʒatse.]

Here's your receipt.	**Вось ваш квіток.** [vɔsʲ vaʃ kvi'tɔk.]
Sorry about the fine.	**Спачуваю наконт штрафу.** [spatʃu'vaʉ na'kɔnt 'ʃtrafu.]
That's okay. It was my fault.	**Гэта нічога. Гэта мая віна.** [ɦɛta ni'tʃɔɦa 'ɦɛta maʲa 'vina.]
Enjoy your trip.	**Прыемнай вам паездкі!** [pri'emnaj vam pa'eztki.]

Taxi

taxi	таксі [tak'si]
taxi driver	таксіст [tak'sist]
to catch a taxi	злавіць таксі [zla'vitsʲ tak'si]
taxi stand	стаянка таксі [sta'ʲanka tak'si]
Where can I get a taxi?	Дзе я магу ўзяць таксі? [dze ʲa ma'ɦu wzʲatsʲ tak'si?]
to call a taxi	выклікаць таксі [viklikatsʲ tak'si]
I need a taxi.	Мне патрэбна таксі. [mne pa'trɛbna tak'si.]
Right now.	Дакладна зараз. [da'kladna 'zaraz.]
What is your address (location)?	Ваш адрас? [vaʃ 'adras?]
My address is …	Мой адрас … [mɔj 'adras …]
Your destination?	Куды вы паедзеце? [ku'di vɨ pa'edzetse?]
Excuse me, …	Прабачце, … [pra'batʃtse, …]
Are you available?	Вы свабодныя? [vɨ sva'bɔdnɨʲa?]
How much is it to get to …?	Колькі каштуе даехаць да …? [kɔlʲki kaʃ'tue da'ehatsʲ da …?]
Do you know where it is?	Вы ведаеце, дзе гэта? [vɨ 'vedaetse, dze 'ɦɛta?]
Airport, please.	У аэрапорт, калі ласка. [u aɛra'pɔrt, ka'li 'laska.]
Stop here, please.	Спыніце тут, калі ласка. [spɨ'nitse tut, ka'li 'laska.]
It's not here.	Гэта ня тут. [ɦɛta nʲa tut.]
This is the wrong address.	Гэта няправільны адрас. [ɦɛta nʲa'pravilʲnɨ 'adras.]

Turn left.

Зараз налева.
[zaraz na'leva.]

Turn right.

Зараз направа.
[zaraz na'prava.]

How much do I owe you?

Колькі я вам павінен /павінна/ заплаціць?
[kɔlʲki ʲa vam pa'vinen /pa'vinna/ zapla'tsitsʲ?]

I'd like a receipt, please.

Дайце мне квіток, калі ласка.
[dajtse mne kvi'tɔk, ka'li 'laska.]

Keep the change.

Рэшты ня трэба.
[rɛʃti nʲa 'trɛba.]

Would you please wait for me?

Пачакайце мяне, калі ласка.
[patʃa'kajtse mʲa'ne, ka'li 'laska.]

five minutes

пяць хвілін
[pʲatsʲ hvi'lin]

ten minutes

дзесяць хвілін
[dzesʲatsʲ hvi'lin]

fifteen minutes

пятнаццаць хвілін
[pʲat'natsatsʲ hvi'lin]

twenty minutes

дваццаць хвілін
[dvatsatsʲ hvi'lin]

half an hour

паўгадзіны
[pawɦa'dzini]

Hotel

Hello.	**Прывітанне.** [privi'tanne.]
My name is …	**Мяне завуць …** [mʲa'ne za'vutsʲ …]
I have a reservation.	**Я зарэзерваваў /зарэзервавала/ нумар.** [ʲa zarɛzerva'vaw /zarɛzerva'vala/ 'numar.]
I need …	**Мне патрэбны …** [mne pa'trɛbnɨ …]
a single room	**аднамесны нумар** [adna'mesnɨ 'numar]
a double room	**двухмесны нумар** [dvuh'mesnɨ 'numar]
How much is that?	**Колькі ён каштуе?** [kɔlʲki ʲon kaʃ'tue?]
That's a bit expensive.	**Гэта крыху дорага.** [ɦɛta 'krihu 'dɔraɦa.]
Do you have anything else?	**У вас ёсць яшчэ што-небудзь?** [u vas ʲostsʲ ʲa'ɕɛ ʃtɔ 'nebutsʲ?]
I'll take it.	**Я вазьму.** [ʲa vazʲ'mu.]
I'll pay in cash.	**Я заплачу наяўнымі.** [ʲa zapla'tʃu naʲawnɨmi.]
I've got a problem.	**У мяне ёсць праблема** [u mʲa'ne ʲostsʲ prab'lema.]
My … is out of order.	**У мяне не працуе …** [u mʲa'ne ne pra'tsue …]
TV	**тэлевізар** [tele'vizar]
air conditioner	**кандыцыянер** [kandɨtsɨʲa'ner]
tap	**кран** [kran]
shower	**душ** [duʃ]
sink	**ракавіна** [rakavina]
safe	**сейф** [sejf]

door lock	замок [za'mɔk]
electrical outlet	разетка [ra'zetka]
hairdryer	фен [fen]

I don't have …	У мяне няма … [u mʲa'ne nʲa'ma …]
water	вады [va'dɨ]
light	святла [svʲat'la]
electricity	электрычнасці [ɛlekt'rɨtʃnasʲtsi]

Can you give me …?	Можаце мне даць …? [mɔʒatse mne datsʲ …?]
a towel	рушнік [ruʃ'nik]
a blanket	коўдру [kɔwdru]
slippers	тапачкі [tapatʃki]
a robe	халат [ha'lat]
shampoo	шампунь [ʃam'punʲ]
soap	мыла [mɨla]

I'd like to change rooms.	Я б хацеў /хацела б/ памяняць нумар. [ʲa b ha'tsew /ha'tsela/ pamʲa'nʲatsʲ 'numar.]
I can't find my key.	Я не магу знайсці свой ключ. [ʲa ne ma'hu znajsʲtsi svɔj klutʃ.]
Could you open my room, please?	Адчыніце мой нумар, калі ласка. [attʃʲi'nitse mɔj 'numar, ka'li 'laska.]
Who's there?	Хто там? [htɔ tam?]
Come in!	Увайдзіце! [uvaj'dzitse!]
Just a minute!	Адну хвіліну! [ad'nu hvi'linu!]
Not right now, please.	Калі ласка, ня зараз. [ka'li 'laska, nʲa 'zaraz.]

Come to my room, please.	Зайдзіце да мяне, калі ласка. [zaj'dzitse da mʲa'ne, ka'li 'laska.]
I'd like to order food service.	Я хачу замовіць ежу ў нумар. [ʲa ha'tʃu za'mɔwitsʲ 'eʒu w 'numar.]

My room number is ...	Нумар майго пакоя ...
	[numar maj'ho pa'kɔʲa ...]
I'm leaving ...	Я з'язджаю ...
	[ʲa zʲaz'dʒau ...]
We're leaving ...	Мы з'язджаем ...
	[mɨ zʲaz'dʒaem ...]
right now	зараз
	[zaraz]
this afternoon	сёння пасля абеду
	[sʲonnʲa pas'lʲa a'bedu]
tonight	сёння ўвечары
	[sʲonnʲa u'wetʃarɨ]
tomorrow	заўтра
	[zawtra]
tomorrow morning	заўтра ўранку
	[zawtra u'ranku]
tomorrow evening	заўтра ўвечары
	[zawtra u'wetʃarɨ]
the day after tomorrow	паслязаўтра
	[paslʲa'zawtra]

I'd like to pay.	Я б хацеў /хацела б/ разлічыцца.
	[ʲa b ha'tsew /ha'tsela/ razli'tʃɨtsa.]
Everything was wonderful.	Усё было выдатна.
	[wsʲo bɨ'lɔ vɨ'datna.]
Where can I get a taxi?	Дзе я магу ўзяць таксі?
	[dze ʲa ma'hu wzʲatsʲ tak'si?]
Would you call a taxi for me, please?	Выклікайце мне таксі, калі ласка.
	[vɨklikajtse mne taksi, ka'li 'laska.]

Restaurant

Can I look at the menu, please?

Магу я паглядзець ваша меню?
[ma'ɦu ja paɦlʲa'dzetsʲ 'vaʃa me'nʉ?]

Table for one.

Столік для аднаго.
[stolik dlʲa adna'ɦɔ.]

There are two (three, four) of us.

Нас два (тры, чатыры) чалавекі.
[nas dva (tri, tʃa'tiri) tʃala'veki.]

Smoking

Для тых, хто паліць.
[dlʲa tih, htɔ 'palitsʲ]

No smoking

Для тых, хто ня паліць.
[dlʲa tih, htɔ nʲa 'palitsʲ]

Excuse me! (addressing a waiter)

Будзьце ласкавы!
[butʲtse las'kavi!]

menu

меню
[me'nʉ]

wine list

карта він
[karta vin]

The menu, please.

Меню, калі ласка.
[me'nʉ, ka'li 'laska.]

Are you ready to order?

Вы гатовы зрабіць замову?
[vi ɦa'tovi zra'bitsʲ za'mɔvu?]

What will you have?

Што вы будзеце замаўляць?
[ʃtɔ vi 'budzetse zamaw'lʲatsʲ?]

I'll have …

Я буду …
[ʲa 'budu …]

I'm a vegetarian.

Я вегетарыянец /вегетарыянка/.
[ʲa veɦetari'ʲanets /veɦetari'ʲanka/.]

meat

мяса
[mʲasa]

fish

рыба
[riba]

vegetables

гародніна
[ɦa'rɔdnina]

Do you have vegetarian dishes?

У вас ёсць вегетарыянскія стравы?
[u vas ʲostsʲ veɦetari'ʲanskiʲa 'stravi?]

I don't eat pork.

Я ня ем свініну.
[ʲa nʲa em svi'ninu.]

He /she/ doesn't eat meat.

Ён /яна/ не есць мяса.
[ʲon /ʲa'na/ ne estsʲ 'mʲasa.]

I am allergic to …

У мяне алергія на …
[u mʲa'ne aler'ɦiʲa na …]

Would you please bring me …

Прынясіце мне, калі ласка …
[prinʲa'sitse mne, ka'li 'laska …]

salt | pepper | sugar

соль | перац | цукар
[sɔlʲ | 'peraʦ | 'ʦukar]

coffee | tea | dessert

каву | гарбату | дэсерт
[kavu | ɦar'batu | dɛ'sert]

water | sparkling | plain

вада | з газам | бяз газу
[va'da | z 'ɦazam | bʲaz 'ɦazu]

a spoon | fork | knife

лыжка | відэлец | нож
[liʒka | vi'dɛleʦ | nɔʒ]

a plate | napkin

талерка | сурвэтка
[ta'lerka | sur'vɛtka]

Enjoy your meal!

Прыемнага апетыту!
[pri'emnaɦa ape'titu!]

One more, please.

Прынясіце яшчэ, калі ласка.
[prinʲa'sitse ʲa'ɕɛ, ka'li 'laska.]

It was very delicious.

Было вельмі смачна.
[bi'lɔ 'velʲmi 'smatʃna.]

---

check | change | tip

рахунак | рэшта | на гарбату
[ra'hunak | 'rɛʃta | na ɦar'batu]

Check, please.
(Could I have the check, please?)

Рахунак, калі ласка.
[ra'hunak, ka'li 'laska.]

Can I pay by credit card?

Магу я заплаціць карткай?
[ma'ɦu ʲa zapla'ʦitsʲ 'kartkaj?]

I'm sorry, there's a mistake here.

Прабачце, тут памылка.
[pra'batʃtse, tut pa'milka.]

Shopping

Can I help you?
Магу я вам дапамагчы?
[ma'ɦu ʲa vam dapamaɦ'ʧi?]

Do you have ...?
У вас ёсць ...?
[u vas ʲosʦʲ ...?]

I'm looking for ...
Я шукаю ...
[ʲa ʃu'kaʉ ...]

I need ...
Мне патрэбны ...
[mne pa'trɛbnɨ ...]

I'm just looking.
Я проста гляджу.
[ʲa 'prosta ɦlʲa'dʒu.]

We're just looking.
Мы проста глядзім.
[mɨ 'prosta ɦlʲa'dzim.]

I'll come back later.
Я зайду пазней.
[ʲa zaj'du paz'nej.]

We'll come back later.
Мы зойдзем пазней.
[mɨ 'zojdzem paz'nej.]

discounts | sale
зніжкі | распродаж
[zniʒki | ras'prodaʒ]

Would you please show me ...
Пакажыце мне, калі ласка ...
[paka'ʒɨʦe mne, ka'li 'laska ...]

Would you please give me ...
Дайце мне, калі ласка ...
[dajʦe mne, ka'li 'laska ...]

Can I try it on?
Магу я гэта прымерыць?
[ma'ɦu ʲa 'ɦɛta pri'meritsʲ?]

Excuse me, where's the fitting room?
Прабачце, дзе прымерачная кабіна?
[pra'baʧʦe, dze pri'meraʧnaʲa ka'bina?]

Which color would you like?
Які колер вы жадаеце?
[ʲaki 'koler vɨ ʒa'daeʦe?]

size | length
памер | рост
[pa'mer | rost]

How does it fit?
Падыйшло?
[padij'ʃlo?]

How much is it?
Колькі гэта каштуе?
[kolʲki 'ɦɛta kaʃ'tue?]

That's too expensive.
Гэта занадта дорага.
[ɦɛta za'natta 'doraɦa.]

I'll take it.
Я вазьму гэта.
[ʲa vazj'mu 'ɦɛta.]

Excuse me, where do I pay?
Прабачце, дзе каса?
[pra'baʧʦe, dze 'kasa?]

Will you pay in cash or credit card?	**Як вы будзеце разлічвацца?** **Наяўнымі ці крэдытнай карткай?** [ˈjak vɨ ˈbudzeʦe razˈliʧvaʦa naˈjawnimi ʦi krɛˈdɨtnaj ˈkartkaj?]
In cash | with credit card	**наяўнымі | карткай** [naˈjawnimi | ˈkartkaj]

Do you want the receipt?	**Вам патрэбен квіток?** [vam paˈtrɛben kviˈtɔk?]
Yes, please.	**Так, будзьце ласкавы.** [tak, ˈbutʲʦe lasˈkavi.]
No, it's OK.	**Не. Не патрэбен. Дзякуй.** [ne, ne paˈtrɛben. ˈdzʲakuj.]
Thank you. Have a nice day!	**Дзякуй. Усяго добрага!** [dzʲakuj. usʲaˈhɔ ˈdɔbraɦa!]

In town

Excuse me, ...	**Прабачце, калі ласка ...** [pra'batʃse, ka'li 'laska ...]
I'm looking for ...	**Я шукаю ...** ['a ʃu'kau ...]
the subway	**метро** [me'trɔ]
my hotel	**сваю гасцініцу** [sva'u ɦas'tsinitsu]
the movie theater	**кінатэатр** [kinatɛ'atr]
a taxi stand	**стаянку таксі** [sta'ʲanku tak'si]
an ATM	**банкамат** [banka'mat]
a foreign exchange office	**пункт абмену валют** [punkt ab'menu va'lut]
an internet café	**інтэрнэт-кафэ** [intɛr'nɛt ka'fɛ]
... street	**вуліцу ...** [vulitsu ...]
this place	**вось гэтае месца** [vɔsʲ 'ɦɛtae 'mesʲtsa]
Do you know where ... is?	**Вы ня ведаеце, дзе знаходзіцца ...?** [vɨ nʲa 'vedaetse, dze zna'ɦɔdzitsa ...?]
Which street is this?	**Як называецца гэтая вуліца?** ['ʲak nazɨ'vaetsa 'ɦɛtaʲa 'vulitsa?]
Show me where we are right now.	**Пакажыце, дзе мы зараз.** [paka'ʒɨtse, dze mɨ 'zaraz.]
Can I get there on foot?	**Я дайду туды пешшу?** ['ʲa daj'du tu'dɨ 'peʃu?]
Do you have a map of the city?	**У вас ёсць карта горада?** [u vas ʲosʲtsʲ 'karta 'ɦɔrada?]
How much is a ticket to get in?	**Колькі каштуе ўваходны білет?** [kɔlʲki kaʃ'tue wva'ɦɔdnɨ bi'let?]
Can I take pictures here?	**Тут дазволена фатаграфаваць?** [tut daz'vɔlena fataɦrafa'vatsʲ?]
Are you open?	**Вы адчынены?** [vɨ at'tʃɨneni?]

When do you open?	**А якой гадзіне вы адчыняецеся?**
	[a ˈjakɔj ɦaˈdzine vɨ atʧɨˈnʲaetsesʲa?]
When do you close?	**Да якой гадзіны вы працуеце?**
	[da ˈjakɔj ɦaˈdzinɨ vɨ praˈtsuetse?]

Money

money	**грошы** [ɦrɔʃi]
cash	**наяўныя грошы** [naˈʲawnʲɪa ˈɦrɔʃi]
paper money	**папяровыя грошы** [papʲaˈrɔvʲɪa ˈɦrɔʃi]
loose change	**дробязь** [drɔbʲazʲ]
check | change | tip	**рахунак | рэшта | на гарбату** [raˈhunak | ˈrɛʃta | na ɦarˈbatu]

credit card	**крэдытная картка** [krɛˈditnaʲa ˈkartka]
wallet	**кашалёк** [kaʃaˈlʲok]
to buy	**купляць** [kupˈlʲatsʲ]
to pay	**плаціць** [plaˈtsitsʲ]
fine	**штраф** [ʃtraf]
free	**бясплатна** [bʲasˈplatna]

Where can I buy ...?	**Дзе я магу купіць ...?** [dze ʲa maˈɦu kuˈpitsʲ ...?]
Is the bank open now?	**Банк зараз адчынены?** [bank ˈzaraz atˈtʃineni?]
When does it open?	**А якой гадзіне ён адчыняецца?** [a ˈʲakɔj ɦaˈdzine ʲon attʃiˈnʲaetsa?]
When does it close?	**Да якой гадзіны ён працуе?** [da ʲaˈkɔj ɦaˈdzini ʲon praˈtsue?]

How much?	**Колькі?** [kɔlʲki?]
How much is this?	**Колькі гэта каштуе?** [kɔlʲki ˈɦɛta kaʃˈtue?]
That's too expensive.	**Гэта занадта дорага.** [ɦɛta zaˈnatta ˈdɔraɦa.]

Excuse me, where do I pay?	**Прабачце, дзе каса?** [praˈbatʃse, dze ˈkasa?]
Check, please.	**Рахунак, калі ласка.** [raˈhunak, kaˈli ˈlaska.]

Can I pay by credit card?

Магу я заплаціць карткай?
[ma'hu ˈa zapla'tsitsʲ 'kartkaj?]

Is there an ATM here?

Тут ёсць банкамат?
[tut ˈostsʲ banka'mat?]

I'm looking for an ATM.

Мне патрэбен банкамат.
[mne pa'trɛben banka'mat.]

I'm looking for a foreign exchange office.

Я шукаю пункт абмену валют.
[ˈa ʃu'kaju punkt ab'menu va'lʉt.]

I'd like to change ...

Я б хацеў /хацела/ памяняць ...
[ˈa b ha'tsew /ha'tsela/ pamʲa'nʲatsʲ ...]

What is the exchange rate?

Які курс абмену?
[ˈaki kurs ab'menu?]

Do you need my passport?

Вам патрэбен мой пашпарт?
[vam pa'trɛben mɔj 'paʃpart?]

Time

What time is it?	**Колькі часу?** [kɔlʲki 'ʧasu?]
When?	**Калі?** [ka'li?]
At what time?	**У колькі?** [u 'kɔlʲki?]
now	later	after …	**зараз	пазней	пасля …** [zaraz	paz'nej	pas'lʲa …]

one o'clock	**гадзіна папоўдні** [ha'dzina pa'pɔwdni]
one fifteen	**гадзіна пятнаццаць** [ha'dzina pʲat'natsatsʲ]
one thirty	**гадзіна трыццаць** [ha'dzina 'tritsatsʲ]
one forty-five	**без пятнаццаці два** [bez pʲat'natsatsi dva]

one	two	three	**адзін	два	тры** [a'dzin	dva	tri]
four	five	six	**чатыры	пяць	шэсць** [ʧa'tiri	pʲatsʲ	ʃɛstsʲ]
seven	eight	nine	**сем	восем	дзевяць** [sem	'vɔsem	'dzevʲatsʲ]
ten	eleven	twelve	**дзесяць	адзінаццаць	дванаццаць** [dzesʲatsʲ	a'dzinatsatsʲ	dva'natsatsʲ]

in …	**праз …** [praz …]
five minutes	**пяць хвілін** [pʲatsʲ hvi'lin]
ten minutes	**дзесяць хвілін** [dzesʲatsʲ hvi'lin]
fifteen minutes	**пятнаццаць хвілін** [pʲat'natsatsʲ hvi'lin]
twenty minutes	**дваццаць хвілін** [dvatsatsʲ hvi'lin]

half an hour	**паўгадзіны** [pawha'dzini]
an hour	**адну гадзіну** [ad'nu ha'dzinu]

in the morning	**раніцай, уранні** [raniʦaj, u'ranni]
early in the morning	**рана ўранні** [rana u'ranni]
this morning	**сёння удзень** [sʲonnʲa u'ʣenʲ]
tomorrow morning	**заўтра раніцай** [zawtra 'raniʦaj]

in the middle of the day	**у абед** [u a'bet]
in the afternoon	**пасля абеду** [pasʲlʲa a'bedu]
in the evening	**увечары** [u'veʧari]
tonight	**сёння увечары** [sʲonnʲa u'veʧari]

at night	**ноччу** [nɔʧu]
yesterday	**учора** [u'ʧora]
today	**сёння** [sʲonnʲa]
tomorrow	**заўтра** [zawtra]
the day after tomorrow	**паслязаўтра** [pasʲlʲa'zawtra]

What day is it today?	**Які сёння дзень?** [ʲaki 'sʲonnʲa ʣenʲ?]
It's …	**Сёння …** [sʲonnʲa …]
Monday	**панядзелак** [panʲa'ʣelak]
Tuesday	**аўторак** [aw'tɔrak]
Wednesday	**серада** [sera'da]

Thursday	**чацвер** [ʧaʦ'ver]
Friday	**пятніца** [pʲatniʦa]
Saturday	**субота** [su'bɔta]
Sunday	**нядзеля** [nʲa'ʣelʲa]

Greetings. Introductions

Hello.	**Прывітанне.** [privi'tanne.]
Pleased to meet you.	**Рады /рада/ з вамі пазнаёміцца.** [radɨ /'rada/ z 'vami pazna'omitsa.]
Me too.	**Я таксама.** [ˈa tak'sama.]
I'd like you to meet …	**Знаёмцеся. Гэта …** [zna'omtses'a. 'ɦɛta …]
Nice to meet you.	**Вельмі прыемна.** [vel'mi pri'emna.]

How are you?	**Як вашы справы?** [ˈak 'vaʃɨ 'spravɨ?]
My name is …	**Мяне завуць …** [mʲa'ne za'vutsʲ …]
His name is …	**Яго завуць …** [ˈaɦɔ za'vutsʲ …]
Her name is …	**Яе завуць …** [ˈae za'vutsʲ …]
What's your name?	**Як вас завуць?** [ˈak vas za'vutsʲ?]
What's his name?	**Як яго завуць?** [ˈak ʲa'ɦɔ za'vutsʲ?]
What's her name?	**Як яе завуць?** [ˈak ʲae za'vutsʲ?]

What's your last name?	**Як ваша прозвішча?** [ˈak 'vaʃa 'prɔzviҫa?]
You can call me …	**Завіце мяне …** [za'vitse mʲa'ne …]
Where are you from?	**Адкуль вы?** [at'kulʲ vɨ]
I'm from …	**Я з …** [ˈa z …]
What do you do for a living?	**Кім вы працуеце?** [kim vɨ pra'tsuetse?]
Who is this?	**Хто гэта?** [htɔ 'ɦɛta?]
Who is he?	**Хто ён?** [htɔ ʲon?]
Who is she?	**Хто яна?** [htɔ ʲa'na?]
Who are they?	**Хто яны?** [htɔ ʲa'nɨ?]

This is …	Гэта …
	[ɦɛta …]
my friend (masc.)	мой сябар
	[mɔj ˈsʲabar]
my friend (fem.)	мая сяброўка
	[maˈʲa sʲabˈrɔwka]
my husband	мой муж
	[mɔj muʒ]
my wife	мая жонка
	[maˈʲa ˈʒɔnka]

my father	мой бацька
	[mɔj ˈbatsʲka]
my mother	мая маці
	[maˈʲa ˈmatsi]
my brother	мой брат
	[mɔj brat]
my sister	мая сястра
	[maˈʲa sʲasˈtra]
my son	мой сын
	[mɔj sin]
my daughter	мая дачка
	[maˈʲa datʃˈka]

This is our son.	Гэта наш сын.
	[ɦɛta naʃ sin.]
This is our daughter.	Гэта наша дачка.
	[ɦɛta ˈnaʃa datʃˈka.]
These are my children.	Гэта мае дзеці.
	[ɦɛta mae ˈdzetsi.]
These are our children.	Гэта нашы дзеці.
	[ɦɛta naʃi ˈdzetsi.]

Farewells

Good bye!	**Да пабачэння!** [da paba'ʧɛnnʲa!]
Bye! (inform.)	**Бывай!** [bi'vaj!]
See you tomorrow.	**Да заўтра.** [da 'zawtra.]
See you soon.	**Да сустрэчы.** [da sus'trɛʧi.]
See you at seven.	**Сустрэнемся ў сем.** [sus'trɛnemsʲa w sem.]

Have fun!	**Баўцеся!** [bawʦesʲa!]
Talk to you later.	**Пагаворым пазней.** [paɦa'vɔrim paz'nej.]
Have a nice weekend.	**Удалых выхадных.** [u'daliɦ viɦad'niɦ.]
Good night.	**Дабранач.** [da'branaʧ.]

It's time for me to go.	**Мне трэба iсцi.** [mne 'trɛba is'ʦi.]
I have to go.	**Мне трэба iсцi.** [mne 'trɛba is'ʦi.]
I will be right back.	**Я зараз вярнуся.** [ʲa 'zaraz vʲar'nusʲa.]

It's late.	**Ужо позна.** [uʒɔ 'pɔzna.]
I have to get up early.	**Мне рана ўставаць.** [mne 'rana wsta'vaʦʲ.]
I'm leaving tomorrow.	**Я заўтра з'язджаю.** [ʲa 'zawtra zʲaz'dʒaʉ.]
We're leaving tomorrow.	**Мы заўтра з'язджаем.** [mɨ 'zawtra zʲaz'dʒaem.]

Have a nice trip!	**Шчаслiвай паездкi!** [ɕas'livaj pa'eztki!]
It was nice meeting you.	**Было прыемна з вамi пазнаёмiцца.** [bi'lɔ pri'emna z 'vami pazna'ʲomiʦa.]
It was nice talking to you.	**Было прыемна з вамi пагутарыць.** [bi'lɔ pri'emna z 'vami pa'ɦutariʦʲ.]
Thanks for everything.	**Дзякуй за ўсё.** [dzʲakuj za 'wsʲo.]

I had a very good time.	**Я цудоўна збавіў /збавіла/ час!** [ˈja tsuˈdɔwna ˈzbawiw /ˈzbawila/ tʃas.]
We had a very good time.	**Мы цудоўна збавілі час!** [mɨ tsuˈdɔwna ˈzbawili tʃas.]
It was really great.	**Усё было выдатна.** [wsʲo bɨˈlɔ vɨˈdatna.]
I'm going to miss you.	**Я буду сумаваць.** [ˈja ˈbudu sumaˈvatsʲ.]
We're going to miss you.	**Мы будзем сумаваць.** [mɨ ˈbudzem sumaˈvatsʲ.]

Good luck!	**Удачы! Шчасліва!** [uˈdatʃi! ɕasˈliva!]
Say hi to …	**Перадавайце прывітанне …** [peradaˈvajtse priviˈtanne …]

Foreign language

I don't understand.	**Я не разумею.** [ˈa ne razuˈmeu̯.]
Write it down, please.	**Напішыце гэта, калі ласка.** [napiˈʂitse ˈɦɛta, kaˈli ˈlaska.]
Do you speak …?	**Вы валодаеце …?** [vɨ vaˈlɔdaetse …?]
I speak a little bit of …	**Я крыху валодаю … мовай** [ˈa ˈkrihu vaˈlɔdau̯ … ˈmɔvaj]
English	**англійскай** [anɦˈlijskaj]
Turkish	**турэцкай** [tuˈrɛtskaj]
Arabic	**арабскай** [aˈrabskaj]
French	**французкай** [franˈtsuskaj]
German	**нямецкай** [nʲaˈmetskaj]
Italian	**італьянскай** [itaˈlʲanskaj]
Spanish	**іспанскай** [isˈpanskaj]
Portuguese	**партугальскай** [partuˈɦalʲskaj]
Chinese	**кітайскай** [kiˈtajskaj]
Japanese	**японскай** [ˈʲaˈpɔnskaj]
Can you repeat that, please.	**Паўтарыце, калі ласка.** [pawtaˈritse, kaˈli ˈlaska.]
I understand.	**Я разумею.** [ˈʲa razuˈmeu̯.]
I don't understand.	**Я не разумею.** [ˈʲa ne razuˈmeu̯.]
Please speak more slowly.	**Гаварыце павольней, калі ласка.** [ɦavaˈritse paˈvɔlʲnej, kaˈli ˈlaska.]
Is that correct? (Am I saying it right?)	**Гэта правільна?** [ɦɛta ˈpravilʲna?]
What is this? (What does this mean?)	**Что гэта?** [tʂtɔ ˈɦɛta?]

Apologies

Excuse me, please.

Выбачайце, калі ласка.
[vɨba'ʧajtse, ka'li 'laska.]

I'm sorry.

Мне шкада.
[mne 'ʃkada.]

I'm really sorry.

Мне вельмі шкада.
[mne 'velʲmi 'ʃkada.]

Sorry, it's my fault.

Я вінаваты /вінавата/, гэта мая віна.
[ʲa vina'vatɨ /vina'vata/, 'hɛta maʲa 'vina.]

My mistake.

Мая памылка.
[maʲa pa'mɨlka.]

May I ...?

Магу я...?
[ma'ɦu ʲa ...?]

Do you mind if I ...?

Вы не будзеце пярэчыць, калі я ...?
[vɨ ne 'budzetse pʲa'rɛʧɨtsʲ, ka'li ʲa ...?]

It's OK.

Нічога страшнага.
[ni'ʧoɦa 'straʃnaɦa.]

It's all right.

Усё ў парадку.
[wsʲo w pa'ratku.]

Don't worry about it.

Не хвалюйцеся.
[ne hva'lʲujtsesʲa.]

Agreement

Yes.	**Так.** [tak.]
Yes, sure.	**Так, канечне.** [tak, ka'netʃne.]
OK (Good!)	**Добра!** [dɔbra!]
Very well.	**Вельмі добра.** [velʲmi 'dɔbra.]
Certainly!	**Канечне!** [ka'netʃne!]
I agree.	**Я згодны /згодна/.** [ʲa 'zɦɔdni /'zɦɔdna/.]

That's correct.	**Дакладна.** [da'kladna.]
That's right.	**Правільна.** [pravilʲna.]
You're right.	**Вы маеце рацыю.** [vi 'maetse 'ratsiu.]
I don't mind.	**Я ня супраць.** [ʲa nʲa 'supratsʲ.]
Absolutely right.	**Зусім дакладна.** [zu'sim da'kladna.]

It's possible.	**Гэта магчыма.** [ɦɛta maɦ'tʃima.]
That's a good idea.	**Гэта добрая думка.** [ɦɛta 'dɔbraʲa 'dumka.]
I can't say no.	**Не магу адмовіць.** [ne ma'ɦu ad'mɔvitsʲ.]
I'd be happy to.	**Буду рады /рада/.** [budu 'radi /'rada/.]
With pleasure.	**З задавальненнем.** [z zadavalʲ'nennem.]

Refusal. Expressing doubt

No.	**Не.** [ne.]
Certainly not.	**Канечне не.** [ka'netʃne ne.]
I don't agree.	**Я не згодны /згодна/.** [ʲa ne 'zɦɔdnɪ /'zɦɔdna/.]
I don't think so.	**Я так не лічу.** [ʲa tak ne liʲtʃu.]
It's not true.	**Гэта няпраўда.** [ɦɛta nʲa'prawda.]

You are wrong.	**Вы памыляецеся.** [vɪ pamɪ'lʲaetsesʲa.]
I think you are wrong.	**Я думаю, што вы памыляецеся.** [ʲa 'dumaʉ, ʃtɔ vɪ pamɪ'lʲaetsesʲa.]
I'm not sure.	**Не ўпэўнены /ўпэўнена/.** [ne u'pɛwnenɪ /u'pɛwnena/.]
It's impossible.	**Гэта немагчыма.** [ɦɛta nemaɦ'tʃɪma.]
Nothing of the kind (sort)!	**Нічога падобнага!** [ni'tʃɔɦa pa'dɔbnaɦa!]

The exact opposite.	**Наадварот!** [naadva'rɔt!]
I'm against it.	**Я супраць.** [ʲa 'supratsʲ.]
I don't care.	**Мне ўсё роўна.** [mne wsʲo 'rɔwna.]

I have no idea.	**Паняцця ня маю.** [pa'nʲatsʲa nʲa 'maʉ.]
I doubt it.	**Сумняваюся, что гэта так.** [sumnʲa'vaʉsʲa, tʃtɔ 'ɦɛta tak.]

Sorry, I can't.	**Прабачце, я не магу.** [pra'batʃtse, ʲa ne ma'ɦu.]
Sorry, I don't want to.	**Прабачце, я не хачу.** [pra'batʃtse, ʲa ne ha'tʃu.]
Thank you, but I don't need this.	**Дзякуй, мне гэта ня трэба.** [dzʲakuj, mne 'ɦɛta nʲa 'trɛba.]
It's getting late.	**Ужо позна.** [uʒɔ 'pɔzna.]

I have to get up early.

Мне рана ўставаць.
[mne 'rana wsta'vatsʲ.]

I don't feel well.

Я дрэнна сябе адчуваю.
[ˈja 'drɛnna sʲa'be attʃu'vau.]

Expressing gratitude

Thank you. **Дзякуй.**
[dzʲakuj.]

Thank you very much. **Дзякуй вялікі!**
[dzʲakuj vʲa'liki.]

I really appreciate it. **Вельмі ўдзячны /удзячна/.**
[welʲmi u'dzʲatʃnɨ /u'dzʲatʃna/.]

I'm really grateful to you. **Я вам удзячны /удзячна/.**
[ʲa vam u'dzʲatʃnɨ /u'dzʲatʃna/.]

We are really grateful to you. **Мы вам удзячны.**
[mɨ vam u'dzʲatʃnɨ.]

Thank you for your time. **Дзякуй, что выдаткавалі час.**
[dzʲakuj, tʃtɔ 'vɨdatkavali tʃas.]

Thanks for everything. **Дзякуй за ўсё.**
[dzʲakuj za 'wsʲo.]

Thank you for ... **Дзякуй за ...**
[dzʲakuj za ...]

your help **вашу дапамогу**
[vaʃu dapa'mɔɦu]

a nice time **прыемныя часіны**
[prɨ'emnʲʲa tʃa'sinɨ]

a wonderful meal **выдатную ежу**
[vɨ'datnuɥ 'eʒu]

a pleasant evening **прыемны вечар**
[prɨ'emnɨ 'vetʃar]

a wonderful day **цудоўны дзень**
[tsu'dɔwnɨ dzenʲ]

an amazing journey **цікавую экскурсію**
[tsi'kavuɥ ɛks'kursiɥ]

Don't mention it. **Няма за што.**
[nʲa'ma za 'ʃtɔ.]

You are welcome. **Ня варта падзякі.**
[nʲa 'varta pa'dzʲaki.]

Any time. **Заўсёды калі ласка.**
[zaw'sʲodɨ ka'li 'laska.]

My pleasure. **Быў рады /Была рада/ дапамагчы.**
[bɨw 'radɨ /bɨla 'rada/ dapamaɦ'tʃɨ.]

Forget it. **Забудзьце. Усё добра.**
[za'butʲtse. wsʲo 'dɔbra.]

Don't worry about it. **Не турбуйцеся.**
[ne tur'bujtsesʲa.]

Congratulations. Best wishes

Congratulations!	**Віншую!** [vin'ʃuʉ!]
Happy birthday!	**З днём нараджэння!** [z 'dnʲom nara'dʒɛnnʲa!]
Merry Christmas!	**Вясёлых Калядаў!** [vʲa'sʲolih ka'lʲadaw!]
Happy New Year!	**С Новым годам!** [s 'nɔvɨm 'hɔdam!]
Happy Easter!	**Са Светлым Вялікаднем!** [sa 'svetlɨm vʲa'likadnem!]
Happy Hanukkah!	**Счаслівай Ханукі!** [stʃas'livaj 'hanuki!]
I'd like to propose a toast.	**У мяне ёсць тост.** [u mʲa'ne ʲostsʲ tɔst.]
Cheers!	**За ваша здароўе!** [za 'vaʃa zda'rɔwe!]
Let's drink to …!	**Вып'ем за …!** [vɨpʲem za …!]
To our success!	**За нашыя поспехі!** [za 'naʃʲʲa 'pɔspehi!]
To your success!	**За вашыя поспехі!** [za 'vaʃʲʲa 'pɔspehi!]
Good luck!	**Удачы!** [u'datʃi!]
Have a nice day!	**Прыемнага вам дня!** [prɨ'emnaɦa vam dnʲa!]
Have a good holiday!	**Добрага вам адпачынку!** [dɔbraɦa vam adpa'tʃinku!]
Have a safe journey!	**Удалай паездкі!** [u'dalaj pa'eztki!]
I hope you get better soon!	**Жадаю вам хуткай папраўкі!** [ʒa'daʉ vam 'hutkaj pa'prawki!]

Socializing

Why are you sad?	**Чаму вы засмучаны?** [ʧa'mu vɨ zas'muʧani?]
Smile! Cheer up!	**Усміхніцеся!** [usmih'niʦesʲa!]
Are you free tonight?	**Вы не занятыя сёння ўвечары?** [vɨ ne za'nʲatɨʲa 'sʲonnʲa u'weʧari?]

May I offer you a drink?	**Магу я прапанаваць вам выпіць?** [ma'hu ʲa prapana'vaʦ vam 'vɨpiʦʲ?]
Would you like to dance?	**Ня хочаце патанцаваць?** [nʲa 'hoʧaʦe patanʦa'vaʦʲ?]
Let's go to the movies.	**Можа сходзім у кіно?** [mɔʒa 'shodzim u ki'nɔ?]

May I invite you to ...?	**Магу я запрасіць вас у ...?** [ma'hu ʲa zapra'siʦʲ vas u ...?]
a restaurant	**рэстаран** [rɛsta'ran]
the movies	**кіно** [ki'nɔ]
the theater	**тэатр** [tɛ'atr]
go for a walk	**на прагулку** [na pra'ɦulku]

At what time?	**У колькі?** [u 'kɔlʲki?]
tonight	**сёння увечары** [sʲonnʲa u'veʧari]
at six	**у шэсць гадзін** [u ʃɛsʦʲ ɦa'dzin]
at seven	**у сем гадзін** [u sem ɦa'dzin]
at eight	**у восем гадзін** [u 'vɔsem ɦa'dzin]
at nine	**у дзевяць гадзін** [u 'dzevʲaʦʲ ɦa'dzin]

Do you like it here?	**Вам тут падабаецца?** [vam tut pada'baeʦa?]
Are you here with someone?	**Вы тут з кімсьці?** [vɨ tut z 'kimsʲʦi?]
I'm with my friend.	**Я з сябрам /сяброўкай/.** [ʲa z 'sʲabram /sʲab'rɔwkaj/.]

I'm with my friends.

Я з сябрамі.
[ˈʲa z sʲab'rami.]

No, I'm alone.

Я адзін /адна/.
[ˈʲa a'dzin /ad'na/.]

Do you have a boyfriend?

У цябе ёсць прыяцель?
[u tsʲa'be ʲostsʲ pri'ʲatselʲ?]

I have a boyfriend.

У мяне ёсць сябар.
[u mʲa'ne ʲostsʲ 'sʲabar.]

Do you have a girlfriend?

У цябе ёсць сяброўка?
[u tsʲa'be ʲostsʲ sʲab'rowka?]

I have a girlfriend.

У мяне ёсць дзяўчына.
[u mʲa'ne ʲostsʲ dzʲaw'tʃina.]

Can I see you again?

Мы яшчэ сустрэнемся?
[mɨ ʲa'ɕɛ sus'trɛnemsʲa?]

Can I call you?

Можна я табе пазваню?
[mɔʒna ʲa ta'be pazva'nʉ?]

Call me. (Give me a call.)

Пазвані мне.
[pazva'ni mne.]

What's your number?

Які ў цябе нумар?
[ʲaki u tsʲa'be 'numar?]

I miss you.

Я сумую па табе.
[ˈʲa su'muʉ pa ta'be.]

You have a beautiful name.

У вас вельмі прыгожае імя.
[u vas 'velʲmi pri'ɦɔʒae i'mʲa.]

I love you.

Я цябе кахаю.
[ˈʲa tsʲa'be ka'haʉ.]

Will you marry me?

Выходзь за мяне замуж.
[vɨ'hɔtsʲ za mʲa'ne 'zamuʒ.]

You're kidding!

Вы жартуеце!
[vɨ ʒar'tuetse!]

I'm just kidding.

Я проста жартую.
[ˈʲa 'prɔsta ʒar'tuʉ.]

Are you serious?

Вы сур'ёзна?
[vɨ su'rʲ)ozna?]

I'm serious.

Я сур'ёзна.
[ˈʲa su'rʲ)ozna.]

Really?!

Сапраўды?!
[sapraw'dɨ?!]

It's unbelievable!

Гэта неверагодна!
[ɦɛta nevera'ɦɔdna]

I don't believe you.

Я вам ня веру.
[ˈʲa vam nʲa 'veru.]

I can't.

Я не магу.
[ˈʲa ne ma'ɦu.]

I don't know.

Я ня ведаю.
[ˈʲa nʲa 'vedaʉ.]

I don't understand you.

Я вас не разумею.
[ˈʲa vas ne razu'meʉ.]

Please go away.	**Сыдзіце, калі ласка.** [sɨ'dzitse, ka'li 'laska.]
Leave me alone!	**Пакіньце мяне у спакоі!** [pa'kinʲtse mʲa'ne u spa'kɔi!]
I can't stand him.	**Я яго не выношу!** [ˈʲa ʲa'ɦɔ ne vɨ'nɔʃu.]
You are disgusting!	**Вы агідныя!** [vɨ a'ɦidnʲiʲa!]
I'll call the police!	**Я выклікаю міліцыю!** [ˈʲa 'vɨklikau̯ mi'litsɨu!]

Sharing impressions. Emotions

I like it.	**Мне гэта падабаецца.** [mne 'ɦɛta pada'baetsa.]
Very nice.	**Вельмі міла.** [velʲmi 'mila.]
That's great!	**Гэта выдатна!** [ɦɛta vɨ'datna!]
It's not bad.	**Гэта някепска.** [ɦɛta nʲa'kepska.]

I don't like it.	**Гэта мне не падабаецца** [ɦɛta mne ne pada'baetsa.]
It's not good.	**Гэта нядобра.** [ɦɛta nʲa'dɔbra.]
It's bad.	**Гэта дрэнна.** [ɦɛta 'drɛnna.]
It's very bad.	**Гэта вельмі дрэнна.** [ɦɛta 'velʲmi 'drɛnna.]
It's disgusting.	**Гэта агідна.** [ɦɛta a'ɦidna.]

I'm happy.	**Я шчаслівы /шчаслівая/.** [ʲa ɕas'livi /ɕas'livaʲa/.]
I'm content.	**Я задаволены /задаволена/.** [ʲa zada'vɔlenɨ /zada'vɔlena/.]
I'm in love.	**Я закаханы /закахана/.** [ʲa zaka'hanɨ /zaka'hana/.]
I'm calm.	**Я спакойны /спакойна/.** [ʲa spa'kɔjnɨ /spa'kɔjna/.]
I'm bored.	**Мне сумна.** [mne 'sumna.]

I'm tired.	**Я стаміўся /стамілася/.** [ʲa sta'miwsʲa /sta'milasʲa/.]
I'm sad.	**Мне нудна.** [mne 'nudna.]
I'm frightened.	**Я напужаны /напужана/.** [ʲa na'puʒanɨ /na'puʒana/.]

I'm angry.	**Я злуюся.** [ʲa zlu'ʉsʲa.]
I'm worried.	**Я хвалююся.** [ʲa hva'lʉjusʲa.]
I'm nervous.	**Я нярвуюся.** [ʲa nʲar'vuʉsʲa.]

I'm jealous. (envious)	**Я зайздрошчу.** [ˈja zajzdˈrɔɕu.]
I'm surprised.	**Я здзіўлены /здзіўлена/.** [ˈja ˈzdʑiwlenɨ /ˈzdʑiwlena/.]
I'm perplexed.	**Я азадачаны /азадачана/.** [ˈja azaˈdatʃanɨ /azaˈdatʃana/.]

Problems. Accidents

I've got a problem.	**У мяне праблема.** [u mʲa'ne prab'lema.]
We've got a problem.	**У нас праблема.** [u nas prab'lema.]
I'm lost.	**Я заблукаў /заблукала/.** [ʲa zablu'kaw /zablu'kala/.]
I missed the last bus (train).	**Я спазніўся на апошні аўтобус (цягнік).** [ʲa spaz'niwsʲa na a'poʃni aw'tɔbus (ʦʲaɦ'nik).]
I don't have any money left.	**У мяне зусім не засталося грошай.** [u mʲa'ne zu'sim ne zasta'losʲa 'ɦrɔʃaj.]

I've lost my …	**Я згубіў /згубіла/…** [ʲa zɦu'biw /zɦu'bila/ …]
Someone stole my …	**У мяне ўкралі …** [u mʲa'ne w'krali …]
passport	**пашпарт** [paʃpart]
wallet	**кашалёк** [kaʃa'lʲok]
papers	**дакументы** [daku'mentɨ]

ticket	**білет** [bi'let]
money	**грошы** [ɦrɔʃɨ]
handbag	**сумку** [sumku]

camera	**фотаапарат** [fɔtaapa'rat]
laptop	**ноутбук** [nɔut'buk]
tablet computer	**планшэт** [plan'ʃɛt]
mobile phone	**тэлефон** [tɛle'fɔn]

Help me!	**Дапамажыце!** [dapama'ʒɨʦe]
What's happened?	**Што здарылася?** [ʃtɔ 'zdarilasʲa?]

fire	пажар [pa'ʒar]
shooting	стралянiна [stralʲa'nina]
murder	забойства [za'bɔjstva]
explosion	выбух [vɨbuh]
fight	бойка [bɔjka]

Call the police!	Выклiкайце мiлiцыю! [vɨklikajʦe mi'liʦiʉ!]
Please hurry up!	Калi ласка, хутчэй! [ka'li 'laska, hu'ʧɛj!]
I'm looking for the police station.	Я шукаю аддзяленне мiлiцыi. [ʲa ʃu'kaʉ adzʲaʲalenne mi'liʦii.]
I need to make a call.	Мне трэба пазванiць. [mne 'trɛba pazva'nitsʲ.]
May I use your phone?	Магу я пазванiць? [ma'ɦu ʲa pazva'nitsʲ?]

I've been …	Мяне … [mʲa'ne …]
mugged	абрабавалi [abraba'vali]
robbed	абкралi [ab'krali]
raped	згвалтавалi [zɦvalta'vali]
attacked (beaten up)	збiлi [zbili]

Are you all right?	З вамi ўсё ў парадку? [z 'vami wsʲo w pa'ratku?]
Did you see who it was?	Вы бачылi, хто гэта быў? [vɨ 'baʧɨli, htɔ 'ɦɛta bɨw?]
Would you be able to recognize the person?	Вы зможаце яго пазнаць? [vɨ 'zmɔʒaʦe ʲa'ɦɔ paz'natsʲ?]
Are you sure?	Вы дакладна ўпэўнены? [vɨ dak'ladna u'pɛwnenɨ?]

Please calm down.	Калi ласка, супакойцеся. [ka'li 'laska, supa'kɔjʦesʲa.]
Take it easy!	Спакайней! [spakaj'nej!]
Don't worry!	Не турбуйцеся. [ne tur'bujʦesʲa.]
Everything will be fine.	Усё будзе добра. [wsʲo 'budze 'dɔbra.]
Everything's all right.	Усё ў парадку. [wsʲo w pa'ratku.]

Come here, please.

Падыдзіце, калі ласка.
[padi'dzitse, ka'li 'laska.]

I have some questions for you.

У мяне да вас некалькі пытанняў.
[u mʲa'ne da vas 'nekalʲki pɨ'tannʲaw.]

Wait a moment, please.

Пачакайце, калі ласка.
[patʃa'kajtse, ka'li 'laska.]

Do you have any I.D.?

У вас ёсць дакументы?
[u vas ʲostsʲ daku'menti?]

Thanks. You can leave now.

Дзякуй. Вы можаце ісці.
[dzʲakuj. vi mɔʒatse isʲtsi.]

Hands behind your head!

Рукі за галаву!
[ruki za ɦala'vu!]

You're under arrest!

Вы арыштаваны.
[vi ariʃta'vani!]

Health problems

Please help me.	**Дапамажыце, калі ласка.** [dapama'ʒiʦe, ka'li 'laska.]
I don't feel well.	**Мне дрэнна.** [mne 'drɛnna.]
My husband doesn't feel well.	**Майму мужу дрэнна.** [majmu 'muʒu 'drɛnna.]
My son ...	**Майму сыну ...** [majmu 'sinu ...]
My father ...	**Майму бацьку ...** [majmu 'baʦʲku ...]
My wife doesn't feel well.	**Маёй жонцы дрэнна.** [maˈoj 'ʒonʦi 'drɛnna.]
My daughter ...	**Маёй дачцэ ...** [maˈoj datʃ'ʦɛ ...]
My mother ...	**Маёй маці ...** [maˈoj 'maʦi ...]
I've got a ...	**У мяне баліць ...** [u mʲa'ne ba'liʦʲ ...]
headache	**галава** [ɦala'va]
sore throat	**горла** [ɦɔrla]
stomach ache	**жывот** [ʒiˈvot]
toothache	**зуб** [zub]
I feel dizzy.	**У мяне кружыцца галава.** [u mʲa'ne 'kruʒiʦa ɦala'va.]
He has a fever.	**У яго тэмпература.** [u ʲa'ɦɔ tɛmpera'tura.]
She has a fever.	**У яе тэмпература.** [u ʲae tɛmpera'tura.]
I can't breathe.	**Я не магу дыхаць.** [ʲa ne ma'ɦu 'dihaʦʲ.]
I'm short of breath.	**Я задыхаюся.** [ʲa zadiˈhauɕa.]
I am asthmatic.	**Я астматык.** [ʲa ast'matik.]
I am diabetic.	**Я дыябетык.** [ʲa diʲa'betik.]

I can't sleep.	**У мяне бяссонніца.** [u mʲaˈne bʲasˈsɔnnitsa.]
food poisoning	**харчовае атручванне** [harˈtʃɔvae atˈrutʃvanne]

It hurts here.	**Баліць вось тут.** [baˈlitsʲ vɔsʲ tut.]
Help me!	**Дапамажыце!** [dapamaˈʒɨtse!]
I am here!	**Я тут!** [ʲa tut!]
We are here!	**Мы тут!** [mɨ tut!]
Get me out of here!	**Выцягніце мяне!** [vɨtsʲaɦnitse mʲaˈne!]
I need a doctor.	**Мне патрэбны доктар.** [mne paˈtrɛbnɨ ˈdɔktar.]
I can't move.	**Я не магу рухацца.** [ʲa ne maˈɦu ˈruɦatsa.]
I can't move my legs.	**Я не адчуваю ног.** [ʲa ne attʃuˈvaʊ nɔɦ.]

I have a wound.	**Я паранены /паранена/.** [ʲa paˈranenɨ /paˈranena/.]
Is it serious?	**Гэта сур'ёзна?** [ɦɛta suˈrʲɔzna?]
My documents are in my pocket.	**Мае дакументы ў кішэні.** [maˈe dakuˈmentɨ w kiˈʃɛni.]
Calm down!	**Супакойцеся!** [supaˈkɔjtsesʲa!]
May I use your phone?	**Магу я пазваніць?** [maˈɦu ʲa pazvaˈnitsʲ?]

Call an ambulance!	**Выклікайце хуткую падамогу!** [vɨklikajtse ˈhutkuʊ padaˈmɔɦu!]
It's urgent!	**Гэта неадкладна!** [ɦɛta neatˈkladna!]
It's an emergency!	**Гэта вельмі неадкладна!** [ɦɛta ˈvelʲmi neatˈkladna!]
Please hurry up!	**Калі ласка, хутчэй!** [kaˈli ˈlaska, huˈtʃɛj!]
Would you please call a doctor?	**Выклікайце доктара, калі ласка!** [vɨklikajtse ˈdɔktara, kaˈli ˈlaska!]
Where is the hospital?	**Скажыце, дзе бальніца?** [skaˈʒɨtse, dze balʲˈnitsa?]

How are you feeling?	**Як вы сябе адчуваеце?** [ʲak vɨ sʲaˈbe attʃuˈvaetse?]
Are you all right?	**З вамі ўсё ў парадку?** [z ˈvami wsʲɔ w paˈratku?]
What's happened?	**Что здарылася?** [tʃtɔ ˈzdarɨlasʲa?]

I feel better now.	**Мне ўжо лепш.** [mne wʒɔ lepʃ.]
It's OK.	**Ўсё ў парадку.** [wsʲo w pa'ratku.]
It's all right.	**Усё добра.** [wsʲo 'dɔbra.]

At the pharmacy

pharmacy (drugstore)	**аптэка** [ap'tɛka]
24-hour pharmacy	**кругласутачная аптэка** [kruɦla'sutaʧnaˡa ap'tɛka]
Where is the closest pharmacy?	**Дзе бліжэйшая аптэка?** [dze bli'ʒɛjʃaˡa ap'tɛka?]
Is it open now?	**Яна зараз адчынена?** [ˡa'na 'zaraz at'ʧinena?]
At what time does it open?	**А якой гадзіне яна адчыняецца?** [a ˡakɔj ɦa'dzine ˡana atʧiˡnˡaeʦa?]
At what time does it close?	**Да якой гадзіны яна працуе?** [da ˡa'kɔj ɦa'dzinɨ ˡa'na pra'ʦue?]
Is it far?	**Гэта далёка?** [ɦɛta da'lˡoka?]
Can I get there on foot?	**Я дайду туды пешшу?** [ˡa daj'du tu'dɨ 'peʃu?]
Can you show me on the map?	**Пакажыце мне на карце, калі ласка.** [paka'ʒɨʦe mne na karʦe, ka'li 'laska.]
Please give me something for …	**Дайце мне чаго-небудзь ад …** [dajʦe mne ʧaɦɔ 'nebutsˡ at …]
a headache	**галаўнога болю** [ɦalaw'nɔɦa 'bolʉ]
a cough	**кашлю** [kaʃlʉ]
a cold	**прастуды** [pra'studɨ]
the flu	**грыпу** [ɦripu]
a fever	**тэмпературы** [tɛmpera'turɨ]
a stomach ache	**болю ў страўніку** [bolʉ w 'strawniku]
nausea	**млоснасці** [mlɔsnasˡʦsi]
diarrhea	**дыярэі** [dˡa'rɛi]
constipation	**запору** [za'pɔru]
pain in the back	**боль у спіне** [bolˡ u spine]

chest pain	боль у грудзях
	[bɔlʲ u ɦru'dzʲah]
side stitch	боль у баку
	[bɔlʲ u ba'ku]
abdominal pain	боль у жываце
	[bɔlʲ u ʒivatse]

pill	таблетка
	[tab'letka]
ointment, cream	мазь, крэм
	[mazʲ, krɛm]
syrup	сіроп
	[si'rɔp]
spray	спрэй
	[sprɛj]
drops	кроплі
	[krɔpli]

You need to go to the hospital.	Вам патрэбна ў бальніцу.
	[vam pa'trɛbna w balʲniʦu.]
health insurance	страхоўка
	[stra'hɔwka]
prescription	рэцэпт
	[rɛ'ʦɛpt]
insect repellant	сродак ад насякомых
	[srɔdak ad nasʲa'kɔmih]
Band Aid	лейкапластыр
	[lejka'plastir]

The bare minimum

Excuse me, ...	**Прабачце, ...** [pra'batʃse, ...]
Hello.	**Прывітанне.** [privi'tanne.]
Thank you.	**Дзякуй.** [dzʲakuj.]
Good bye.	**Да пабачэння.** [da paba'tʃɛnnʲa.]
Yes.	**Так.** [tak.]
No.	**Не.** [ne.]
I don't know.	**Я ня ведаю.** [ˈʲa nʲa 'vedau.]
Where? | Where to? | When?	**Дзе? | Куды? | Калі?** [dze? | ku'dɨ? | ka'li?]
I need ...	**Мне трэба ...** [mne 'trɛba ...]
I want ...	**Я хачу ...** [ˈʲa ha'tʃu ...]
Do you have ...?	**У вас ёсць ...?** [u vas ʲostsʲ ...?]
Is there a ... here?	**Тут ёсць ...?** [tut ʲostsʲ ...?]
May I ...?	**Я магу ...?** [ˈʲa ma'hu ...?]
..., please (polite request)	**Калі ласка** [ka'li 'laska]
I'm looking for ...	**Я шукаю ...** [ˈʲa ʃu'kau ...]
the restroom	**туалет** [tua'let]
an ATM	**банкамат** [banka'mat]
a pharmacy (drugstore)	**аптэку** [ap'tɛku]
a hospital	**бальніцу** [balj'nitsu]
the police station	**аддзяленне міліцыі** [adzʲa'lenne mi'litsii]
the subway	**метро** [me'trɔ]

a taxi	таксі
	[tak'si]
the train station	вакзал
	[vak'zal]

My name is …	Мяне завуць …
	[mʲaˈne zaˈvuʦʲ …]
What's your name?	Як вас завуць?
	[ʲak vas zaˈvuʦʲ?]
Could you please help me?	Дапамажыце мне, калі ласка.
	[dapamaˈʒiʦe mne, kaˈli ˈlaska?]
I've got a problem.	У мяне праблема.
	[u mʲaˈne prabˈlema.]
I don't feel well.	Мне дрэнна.
	[mne ˈdrɛnna.]
Call an ambulance!	Выклікайце хуткую дапамогу!
	[viklikajʦe ˈhutkuʉ dapaˈmɔɦu!]
May I make a call?	Магу я пазваніць?
	[maˈɦu ʲa pazvaˈniʦʲ?]

I'm sorry.	Выбачце.
	[vibatʃse.]
You're welcome.	Калі ласка.
	[kaˈli ˈlaska.]

I, me	я [ʲa]
you (inform.)	ты [ti]
he	ён [ʲon]
she	яна [ʲaˈna]
they (masc.)	яны [ʲaˈni]
they (fem.)	яны [ʲaˈni]
we	мы [mi]
you (pl)	вы [vi]
you (sg, form.)	вы [vi]

ENTRANCE	УВАХОД [uvaˈhɔd]
EXIT	ВЫХАД [viˈhad]
OUT OF ORDER	НЕ ПРАЦУЕ [ne praˈʦue]
CLOSED	ЗАЧЫНЕНА [zaˈʧinena]

OPEN	**АДЧЫНЕНА**
	[at'ʧinena]
FOR WOMEN	**ДЛЯ ЖАНЧЫН**
	[dlʲa ʒan'ʧin]
FOR MEN	**ДЛЯ МУЖЧЫН**
	[dlʲa muʒ'ʧin]

T&P BOOKS

MINI DICTIONARY

This section contains 250
useful words required for
everyday communication.
You will find the names of
months and days of the week
here. The dictionary also
contains topics such as colors,
measurements, family, and
more

T&P Books Publishing

DICTIONARY CONTENTS

T&P Books Publishing

time	час (м)	['tʃas]
hour	гадзіна (ж)	[ɦaˈdzina]
half an hour	паўгадзіны	[pawɦaˈdzinɨ]
minute	хвіліна (ж)	[hviˈlina]
second	секунда (ж)	[seˈkunda]
today (adv)	сёння	[ˈsʲonnʲa]
tomorrow (adv)	заўтра	[ˈzawtra]
yesterday (adv)	учора	[uˈtʃɔra]
Monday	панядзелак (м)	[panʲaˈdzelak]
Tuesday	аўторак (м)	[awˈtorak]
Wednesday	серада (ж)	[seraˈda]
Thursday	чацвер (м)	[tʃatsˈver]
Friday	пятніца (ж)	[ˈpʲatnitsa]
Saturday	субота (ж)	[suˈbota]
Sunday	нядзеля (ж)	[nʲaˈdzelʲa]
day	дзень (м)	[ˈdzenʲ]
working day	працоўны дзень (м)	[praˈtsownɨ ˈdzenʲ]
public holiday	святочны дзень (м)	[svʲaˈtɔtʃnɨ ˈdzenʲ]
weekend	выхадныя (м мн)	[vɨhadˈnʲia]
week	тыдзень (м)	[ˈtɨdzenʲ]
last week (adv)	на мінулым тыдні	[na miˈnulɨm ˈtɨdni]
next week (adv)	на наступным тыдні	[na naˈstupnɨm ˈtɨdni]
in the morning	ранкам	[ˈrankam]
in the afternoon	пасля абеду	[paˈslʲa aˈbedu]
in the evening	увечар	[uˈvetʃar]
tonight (this evening)	сёння ўвечары	[ˈsʲonnʲa uˈwetʃarɨ]
at night	уначы	[unaˈtʃɨ]
midnight	поўнач (ж)	[ˈpownatʃ]
January	студзень (м)	[ˈstudzenʲ]
February	люты (м)	[ˈlʉtɨ]
March	сакавік (м)	[sakaˈvik]
April	красавік (м)	[krasaˈvik]
May	май (м)	[ˈmaj]
June	чэрвень (м)	[ˈtʃɛrvenʲ]
July	ліпень (м)	[ˈlipenʲ]
August	жнівень (м)	[ˈʒnivenʲ]

September	верасень (м)	['verasenʲ]
October	кастрычнік (м)	[kas'trit͡ʃnik]
November	лістапад (м)	[lista'pat]
December	снежань (м)	['sneʒanʲ]

in spring	увесну	[u'vesnu]
in summer	улетку	[u'letku]
in fall	увосень	[u'vɔsenʲ]
in winter	узімку	[u'zimku]

month	месяц (м)	['mesʲat͡s]
season (summer, etc.)	сезон (м)	[se'zɔn]
year	год (м)	['ɦɔt]

2. Numbers. Numerals

0 zero	нуль (м)	['nulʲ]
1 one	адзін	[a'dzin]
2 two	два	['dva]
3 three	тры	['tri]
4 four	чатыры	[t͡ʃa'tiri]

5 five	пяць	['pʲat͡sʲ]
6 six	шэсць	['ʃɛst͡sʲ]
7 seven	сем	['sem]
8 eight	восем	['vɔsem]
9 nine	дзевяць	['dzevʲat͡sʲ]
10 ten	дзесяць	['dzesʲat͡sʲ]

11 eleven	адзінаццаць	[adzi'nat͡sat͡sʲ]
12 twelve	дванаццаць	[dva'nat͡sat͡sʲ]
13 thirteen	трынаццаць	[tri'nat͡sat͡sʲ]
14 fourteen	чатырнаццаць	[t͡ʃatir'nat͡sat͡sʲ]
15 fifteen	пятнаццаць	[pʲat'nat͡sat͡sʲ]

16 sixteen	шаснаццаць	[ʃas'nat͡sat͡sʲ]
17 seventeen	семнаццаць	[sʲam'nat͡sat͡sʲ]
18 eighteen	васемнаццаць	[vasʲam'nat͡sat͡sʲ]
19 nineteen	дзевятнаццаць	[dzevʲat'nat͡sat͡sʲ]

20 twenty	дваццаць	['dvat͡sat͡sʲ]
30 thirty	трыццаць	['trit͡sat͡sʲ]
40 forty	сорак	['sɔrak]
50 fifty	пяцьдзесят	[pʲadzʲa'sʲat]

60 sixty	шэсцьдзесят	['ʃɛzʲdzesʲat]
70 seventy	семдзесят	['semdzesʲat]
80 eighty	восемдзесят	['vɔsemdzesʲat]
90 ninety	дзевяноста	[dzevʲa'nɔsta]
100 one hundred	сто	['stɔ]

200 two hundred	дзвесце	[dzj'vesʲtse]
300 three hundred	трыста	['trista]
400 four hundred	чатырыста	[tʃa'tirista]
500 five hundred	пяцьсот	[pʲatsʲsot]

600 six hundred	шэсцьсот	[ʃɛstsʲ'sot]
700 seven hundred	семсот	[sem'sot]
800 eight hundred	восемсот	[vosem'sot]
900 nine hundred	дзевяцьсот	[dzevʲatsʲ'sot]
1000 one thousand	тысяча	['tisʲatʃa]

| 10000 ten thousand | дзесяць тысяч | ['dzesʲatsʲ 'tisʲatʃ] |
| one hundred thousand | сто тысяч | ['stɔ 'tisʲatʃ] |

| million | мільён (м) | [mi'lʲjɔn] |
| billion | мільярд (м) | [mi'lʲart] |

3. Humans. Family

man (adult male)	мужчына (м)	[mu'ʃɕina]
young man	юнак (м)	[ʉ'nak]
woman	жанчына (ж)	[ʒan'tʃina]
girl (young woman)	дзяўчына (ж)	[dzʲaw'tʃina]
old man	стары (м)	[sta'ri]
old woman	старая (ж)	[sta'raʲa]

mother	маці (ж)	['matsi]
father	бацька (м)	['batsʲka]
son	сын (м)	['sin]
daughter	дачка (ж)	[datʃ'ka]
brother	брат (м)	['brat]
sister	сястра (ж)	[sʲast'ra]

parents	бацькі (мн)	[batsʲ'ki]
child	дзіця (н)	[dzi'tsʲa]
children	дзеці (н мн)	['dzetsi]
stepmother	мачаха (ж)	['matʃaha]
stepfather	айчым (м)	[aj'tʃim]

grandmother	бабуля (ж)	[ba'bulʲa]
grandfather	дзядуля (м)	[dzʲa'dulʲa]
grandson	унук (м)	[u'nuk]
granddaughter	унучка (ж)	[u'nutʃka]
grandchildren	унукі (м мн)	[u'nuki]

uncle	дзядзька (м)	['dzʲatsʲka]
aunt	цётка (ж)	['tsʲotka]
nephew	пляменнік (м)	[plʲa'mennik]
niece	пляменніца (ж)	[plʲa'mennitsa]
wife	жонка (ж)	['ʒɔnka]

husband	муж (м)	['muʃ]
married (masc.)	жанаты	[ʒa'nati]
married (fem.)	замужняя	[za'muʒnæʲa]
widow	удава (ж)	[u'dava]
widower	удавец (м)	[uda'vets]

| name (first name) | імя (н) | [i'mʲa] |
| surname (last name) | прозвішча (н) | ['prozʲviʃca] |

relative	сваяк (м)	[sva'ʲak]
friend (masc.)	сябар (м)	['sʲabar]
friendship	сяброўства (н)	[sʲab'rowstva]

partner	партнёр (м)	[part'nʲor]
superior (n)	начальнік (м)	[na'tʃalʲnik]
colleague	калега (м, ж)	[ka'leɦa]
neighbors	суседзі (м мн)	[su'sedzi]

4. Human body

body	цела (н)	['tsela]
heart	сэрца (н)	['sɛrtsa]
blood	кроў (ж)	['krow]
brain	мозг (м)	['mosk]

bone	косць (ж)	['kostsʲ]
spine (backbone)	пазваночнік (м)	[pazva'notʃnik]
rib	рабро (н)	[rab'ro]
lungs	лёгкія (н мн)	['lʲoɦkiʲa]
skin	скура (ж)	['skura]

head	галава (ж)	[ɦala'va]
face	твар (м)	['tvar]
nose	нос (м)	['nos]
forehead	лоб (м)	['lop]
cheek	шчака (ж)	[ʃca'ka]

mouth	рот (м)	['rot]
tongue	язык (м)	[ʲa'zik]
tooth	зуб (м)	['zup]
lips	губы (ж мн)	['ɦubi]
chin	падбародак (м)	[padba'rodak]

ear	вуха (н)	['vuha]
neck	шыя (ж)	['ʃiʲa]
eye	вока (н)	['voka]
pupil	зрэнка (ж)	['zrɛnka]
eyebrow	брыво (н)	[bri'vo]
eyelash	вейка (ж)	['vejka]
hair	валасы (м мн)	[vala'si]

hairstyle	прычоска (ж)	[pri'tʃɔska]
mustache	вусы (м мн)	['vusi̯]
beard	барада (ж)	[bara'da]
to have (a beard, etc.)	насіць	[na'sitsʲ]
bald (adj)	лысы	['lisi̯]

hand	кісць (ж)	['kistsʲ]
arm	рука (ж)	[ru'ka]
finger	палец (м)	['palets]
nail	пазногаць (м)	[paz'nɔɦatsʲ]
palm	далонь (ж)	[da'lɔnʲ]

shoulder	плячо (н)	[plʲa'tʃɔ]
leg	нага (ж)	[na'ɦa]
knee	калена (н)	[ka'lena]
heel	пятка (ж)	['pʲatka]
back	спіна (ж)	['spina]

5. Clothing. Personal accessories

clothes	адзенне (н)	[a'dzenne]
coat (overcoat)	паліто (н)	[pali'tɔ]
fur coat	футра (н)	['futra]
jacket (e.g., leather ~)	куртка (ж)	['kurtka]
raincoat (trenchcoat, etc.)	плашч (м)	['plaʃt͡ɕ]

shirt (button shirt)	кашуля (ж)	[ka'ʃulʲa]
pants	штаны (мн)	[ʃta'ni̯]
suit jacket	пінжак (м)	[pin'ʒak]
suit	касцюм (м)	[kas'tsɵm]

dress (frock)	сукенка (ж)	[su'kenka]
skirt	спадніца (ж)	[spad'nitsa]
T-shirt	футболка (ж)	[fud'bɔlka]
bathrobe	халат (м)	[ha'lat]
pajamas	піжама (ж)	[pi'ʒama]
workwear	працоўнае адзенне (н)	[pra'tsɔwnae a'dzenne]

underwear	бялізна (ж)	[bʲa'lizna]
socks	шкарпэткі (ж мн)	[ʃkar'pɛtki]
bra	бюстгальтар (м)	[bɵz'ɦalʲtar]
pantyhose	калготкі (мн)	[kal'ɦɔtki]
stockings (thigh highs)	панчохі (ж мн)	[pan'tʃɔhi]
bathing suit	купальнік (м)	[ku'palʲnik]

hat	шапка (ж)	['ʃapka]
footwear	абутак (м)	[a'butak]
boots (e.g., cowboy ~)	боты (м мн)	['bɔti]
heel	абцас (м)	[ap'tsas]
shoestring	шнурок (м)	[ʃnu'rɔk]

shoe polish	крэм (м) для абутку	['krɛm dlʲa a'butku]
gloves	пальчаткі (ж мн)	[palʲ'tʃatki]
mittens	рукавіцы (ж мн)	[ruka'vitsi]
scarf (muffler)	шалік (м)	['ʃalik]
glasses (eyeglasses)	акуляры (мн)	[aku'lʲari]
umbrella	парасон (м)	[para'sɔn]

tie (necktie)	гальштук (м)	['halʲʃtuk]
handkerchief	насоўка (ж)	[na'sɔwka]
comb	грабянец (м)	[hrabʲa'nets]
hairbrush	шчотка (ж) для валасоў	['ʃɕɔtka dlʲa vala'sɔw]

buckle	спражка (ж)	['spraʃka]
belt	пояс (м)	['pɔʲas]
purse	сумачка (ж)	['sumatʃka]

6. House. Apartment

apartment	кватэра (ж)	[kva'tɛra]
room	пакой (м)	[pa'kɔj]
bedroom	спальня (ж)	['spalʲnʲa]
dining room	сталоўка (ж)	[sta'lɔwka]

living room	гасцёўня (ж)	[has'tsʲownʲa]
study (home office)	кабінет (м)	[kabi'net]
entry room	вітальня (ж)	[vi'talʲnʲa]
bathroom (room with a bath or shower)	ванны пакой (м)	['vanni pa'kɔj]
half bath	прыбіральня (ж)	[pribi'ralʲnʲa]

vacuum cleaner	пыласос (м)	[pila'sɔs]
mop	швабра (ж)	['ʃvabra]
dust cloth	ануча (ж)	[a'nutʃa]
short broom	венік (м)	['venik]
dustpan	шуфлік (м) для смецця	['ʃuflik dlʲa 'smetsʲa]

furniture	мэбля (ж)	['mɛblʲa]
table	стол (м)	['stɔl]
chair	крэсла (н)	['krɛsla]
armchair	фатэль (м)	[fa'tɛlʲ]

mirror	люстэрка (н)	[lʉs'tɛrka]
carpet	дыван (м)	[di'van]
fireplace	камін (м)	[ka'min]
drapes	шторы (мн)	['ʃtɔri]
table lamp	настольная лямпа (ж)	[na'stɔlʲnaʲa 'lʲampa]
chandelier	люстра (ж)	['lʉstra]

kitchen	кухня (ж)	['kuhnʲa]
gas stove (range)	пліта (ж) газавая	[pli'ta 'hazavaʲa]

electric stove	пліта (ж) электрычная	[pli'ta ɛlekt'ritʃnaʲa]
microwave oven	мікрахвалевая печ (ж)	[mikra'hvalevaʲa 'petʃ]
refrigerator	халадзільнік (м)	[hala'dzilʲnik]
freezer	маразілка (ж)	[mara'zilka]
dishwasher	пасудамыечная машына (ж)	[pasuda'mietʃnaʲa ma'ʃina]
faucet	кран (м)	['kran]
meat grinder	мясарубка (ж)	[mʲasa'rupka]
juicer	сокавыціскалка (ж)	[sɔkavitsi'skalka]
toaster	тостэр (м)	['tɔstɛr]
mixer	міксер (м)	['mikser]
coffee machine	кававарка (ж)	[kava'varka]
kettle	чайнік (м)	['tʃajnik]
teapot	імбрычак (м)	[im'britʃak]
TV set	тэлевізар (м)	[tɛle'vizar]
VCR (video recorder)	відэамагнітафон (м)	['vidɛa maɦnita'fɔn]
iron (e.g., steam ~)	прас (м)	['pras]
telephone	тэлефон (м)	[tɛle'fɔn]

www.ingramcontent.com/pod-product-compliance
Lightning Source LLC
Chambersburg PA
CBHW070841050426
42452CB00011B/2370